Ten Teachings

for

One World

TEN TEACHINGS
for ONE WORLD

Wisdom from Mother Mary

GINA LAKE

Endless Satsang Foundation

www.RadicalHappiness.com

ISBN: 978-1724663900

Cover photo: © Anthony Baggett/Dreamstime.com
Copyright © 2013 by Gina Lake

CONTENTS

INTRODUCTION

It was a sunny autumn day, and I was on a spiritual retreat among magnificent old trees and green, grassy trails that meandered through many acres of colorful woods. In a special spot on this property, stood a small statue of Mother Mary, surrounded by mossy rocks and foliage, like a beautiful little grotto. I sat down in front of the statue on a stone bench. I've always loved Mother Mary. As a child, I felt comforted by her, and although I'm no longer a Catholic, I still love seeing statues and images of her.

My mind was especially still that morning because I'd been meditating for five days. I drank in the beauty and stillness of that moment, which permeated my being. As I sat looking at Mother Mary, the light shifted, as if coming from another dimension, and the statue seemed to come alive. The face, with eyes cast down, suddenly changed, and

Mother Mary's eyes opened and looked at me. This startled me, and I became transfixed by the vision in front of me.

Then I heard Mother Mary speak. Her voice was gentle and non-imposing: "You are my beloved child." The voice was clear and resonant within my mind, and her gentle energy enveloped me. The voice was very feminine but womanly and grounded. Mother Mary spoke to me lovingly and mentioned that she might like me to write down some messages for her sometime but that she wouldn't ask that of me until we got to know each other first.

After this meeting, I felt a tingle of light pouring in the top of my head, which I took as a blessing from her. Over the following months whenever I spoke with Mother Mary, my state of consciousness was deeply affected for hours. And now, nine months since our first meeting, as I finish writing this book, I feel her energy with me. Writing it has been a gift to me, and I hope that her energy is something you'll be able to feel as well while you read these words. It is the energy of peace.

It isn't important that you believe where the words in this book came from. I'm sharing this story with you only because this was how these teachings came to be written. As with all words, no matter where they come from, what's important is whether they ring true in your own being and whether they bring you closer to love and peace, which is my purpose in writing this. If words do the opposite, then they are worse than useless.

Having said that, I invite you to share in the ten teachings that follow. The teachings are intended to bring us into closer contact with the peace and love that is our divine nature, which has the capacity to transform our hearts and our world.

Gina Lake
August, 2013

PREFACE

I am Mother Mary, and I am offering these ten teachings to you now in this way, because I have the opportunity to work through this individual, Gina Lake, who has the vocabulary, understanding, and readers I wish to reach. What I "paint" through this instrument will be different than what I "paint" though another. It will be, in part, an expression of the instrument. Just as an artist is influenced by the medium he or she is working in, so am I. And just as the artist freely chooses the instrument for a reason, so have I. The language and teachings are tailored to her readers for the purpose of furthering their enlightenment. Ultimately, my purpose, as always, is to foster peace on earth. These are times that require such teachings and times in which there is a readiness to receive them. Thank you for being open to receiving these teachings. So, let us begin.

The First Teaching

Open and Receive

Of all the creatures on this beautiful earth, only human beings are blessed with the potential of awareness of their divine nature. Other creatures know the Divine in their own way, but you can know yourselves *as* the Divine. And that is the design, to create beings who will one day awaken to their divinity within the human condition. This is the plan, and it is an exquisite one, carried out throughout the galaxy, indeed, throughout the universe: to create sentient beings who will one day discover the secret of their own creation—where they came from and who they truly are.

These are special times, indeed, as so many are waking up to the knowledge that has been hidden away, stored in your DNA, for just such a time. You are blessed to be one who is being guided to look beyond your human self to the divinity within.

These are exciting *and* dangerous times, as you are confronted daily by misconceptions, wrong ideas, negative thoughts, even negative entities, which seek to pull you off your track of discovery, of recovery of your precious divine self. You are tossed to and fro by the many influences, some very, very convincing, that bring you deeper into the illusion of being separate from the Divine and at odds with other human beings.

The world has come to a crossroads, and it must choose. It can move forward on the basis of the old paradigm of separation, hatred, and conflict or on the basis of a new one that acknowledges your divinity and Oneness with all of creation, including the many beings who have been watching over you and guiding your evolution.

Yes, you are deeply loved, and this love is proven by the careful and painstaking guidance each and every one of you is being given every second of your life. Do you know this? Do you know how very loved and looked after you are? You are the treasured fruit of this dear planet, and we love and cherish you and every living form that makes your life possible.

It is so important that you know this now. So many of you feel abandoned and at the mercy of a hostile and dangerous world. But not a single one of you has ever been abandoned. Rather, some have abandoned their belief in goodness, in the guidance and love that are showered upon them. And in rejecting a belief in such gifts, they do not experience them. They cut themselves off from them and from their divine inheritance. Only they can change this. Only they can decide to recognize and receive this inheritance, for it is not for those guiding humanity to foist it upon you. You only need to see that love and guidance are already present in every moment for this to be your experience and your reality.

If you find this love and guidance difficult to perceive, then merely express your openness to perceiving and receiving it. Do not say "I can't feel it," because that is like saying "I won't feel it," and so you won't. Instead say "I am willing to feel it," and then feeling it will become a reality. This is so important and it is easy.

As easy as it is to make such a statement of openness and willingness, it still must be made for many of you to be able to feel what is being given to you. A lack of openness is often the only block to connecting with your Source, your divine nature, and the bounty that accrues from that. The only block. Life is this beneficent. Like Dorothy's ruby slippers, which could always have taken her home to Kansas, your knowledge of the truth and willingness to receive all that is being given to you is all you have ever needed to return Home.

So, this is my first teaching: *Open and you will receive.* I do not mean you will receive whatever your humanness wants but that you will receive what your inner divinity—your soul—wants. And that is what you really want. What your humanness, or ego, wants are not true desires but manufactured ones, which often take you away from your deepest desire. The game that humanity is playing is created this way: You have desires that take you away from what you really want.

How long will it take to unmask this game? Some people take eons, while others do not take as long. It is up to you. You get to play the game however you wish. By going after your ego's desires, you will have many experiences and much drama. That can be exciting and fun, just as other games in which you struggle, strive, and win and lose can be quite fun. But at a certain point, you tire of these games and long for the peace at your very core. You long to go Home.

Many of you are ready to do that now. Many are at this point, where the game has worn itself out and you are ready for peace. You see that peace was what was lacking in the game of desire, and now you want peace.

Whole worlds get to this point in their evolution, just as individuals do. A world eventually tires of struggle, strife, and drama. When that happens, those who foment hatred and war no longer have the power to get others to follow them. Your world will get to this point someday, and it will arrive because individuals have found peace within themselves and no longer accept anything but peace.

What keeps you from believing in the goodness of life, in the unending stream of love and support that flow to you from other dimensions? This stream is experienced by those who are willing to open to and receive its bounty. If you are not open to this stream and drinking from it as fully as you can, then what beliefs keep you from doing so? It is only on your end that the flow can be obstructed. Your beliefs are all that stand in the way of experiencing the beneficence of life and the guidance that is available to you. What do you believe about life, about God? What do you believe about yourself?

The most common obstacle to receiving this Grace is feeling unworthy. Can you accept the love that is offered to you? If as a child you were not loved adequately, then receiving love in any form, including Grace, is likely to be difficult. To break through this block, all that is needed is a *willingness* to receive. In this willingness lies the potential to see the truth about who you really are. Once you open to Grace, you receive Grace and discover the truth—that you belong to Oneness and therefore cannot be anything but loved and cherished.

The reason it is so important that you feel loved is so that you can love more freely. Be willing to accept the love that is being showered on you from other dimensions so that you can become the loving being that you are meant to be. Love is your destiny.

Any idea you might have about not being loved, cared for, and cherished is just an idea—a wisp of your imagination—that holds no truth. You make up that idea, and you can also discard it and replace it with the truth. You are powerful creators of your reality in this way. You declare what you believe, and then that becomes your experience until you declare something else.

It may be true that you weren't loved and cared for sufficiently as a child, but that experience is gone. Now all you have left is your story about that, your sense of being someone who is not lovable, and your feeling that life is not caring. This story and these feelings are not real. You made them up, and you can give them up once you see the illusion you have cast. However, only you can un-tell the story and dissolve the illusion, because it is your creation.

Human beings are playing at being creators. That is the purpose of human creation: to explore creation by creating and, in the process, to evolve. Creation is a grand experiment of discovery and evolution, not only for humans, but also for the Divine. It created you as part of its exploration and evolution.

True enjoyment of life is possible when you open to the possibility that this is what is going on. You are not a victim of a cruel world but a willing participant and an adventurer faced with all manner of challenges, all of which can be overcome, if not actually, then at least internally. Every challenge can be won with the proper attitudinal shift, with a shift in consciousness. Every difficulty can be used to make you stronger when approached from the consciousness of Oneness. And that is what you are here to achieve: an awareness of your oneness with all in the midst of this experience of duality, this earthly life.

You are a spiritual being with an enormous capacity for love, who is capable of radiating peace and serving others out of pure adoration of the life they represent. When you are in touch with your true nature, you happily and naturally serve others, for your needs are few and your energy is abundant.

This level of service is only possible when you know that others are indeed your very own self. When you know, "I am you and you and also you," then all selfishness disappears. You serve others because it feels good to do so and to not do so would not feel good. In truth, it always felt good to serve others, but when you had many desires and needs that seemed to compete with other people's, serving others didn't make sense. To the ego, serving oneself is the only thing that makes sense.

At a certain point in your spiritual evolution, the ego weakens, which allows something else to shine forth. Many of you are at that point now. The ego has shown itself to be false, misleading, and unreliable, and you are ready for a new master. Then something truer steps forward and becomes obvious. It has always been there, behind the scenes, even running the show much of the time without your awareness.

Once you wake up from having been hypnotized by the ego, the false self, you can choose whether the false self or the true one controls your speech and actions. When the truth is seen clearly—that the false self has been leading and that that is not necessary nor desirable—that is a momentous time in one's evolution. Something else is here and has always been here, awake and alive in you, ready to move you instead of the false self.

For this transformation to happen, you have to be willing to see yourself differently. You have to be willing to see yourself as the magnificent and loving being that you are and can be. Are you willing? What beliefs keep you from being willing to see yourself this way? How do you see yourself? Do you realize that that is an imagination? You made that up, possibly with the help of others who told you who and what you are.

Why not imagine something grander, something much truer, and that will become your experience. This is how you awaken from the illusion of being limited, small, inadequate, less than. Be willing to see yourself as the divine being that you truly are— and you will be! That is the promise. You can be what you truly are when you open to that possibility and are willing to know yourself as that.

THE SECOND TEACHING

Acknowledge the Hand of Grace

You are more precious than you realize. There is no one else like you anywhere in the universe. Human beings are unique, and each of you is a unique human being, although you are not actually a human being but just playing one for a time. You are a divine spark that has taken the form of a human being. You will one day shed this persona and become the light-being that you are.

Like a caterpillar that turns into a butterfly, your current form does not adequately reflect your majesty and potential. The caterpillar cannot conceive of flying, and like the caterpillar, you cannot conceive of what you will become and are becoming, for even now you are changing. This transformation is setting the stage for a much larger transformation to come. Nevertheless, the caterpillar is not inferior to the butterfly; it is just different. The Divine has a plan for each of you and for humanity as a whole. Every step of the plan is perfect and equally valued by the Creator, so there is no need to hurry through a stage to get to the next or to disparage one stage and elevate another.

There is nothing that is apart from the Divine's care and consideration. The Divine has a hand in even the smallest aspect of creation. It has a plan for each and everything it has created, and it guides the unfolding of this plan. The hand of God within creation is often called Grace. It can appear accidental, capricious, or purposeless, but always this hand moves with wisdom, love, and in accordance with a greater scheme. That is not to say that terrible things do not happen that are not the hand of God, for the hand of humankind produces terrible results at times, and this is allowed as part of the plan.

The Grace of God is seen in the movement of the stars, the perfection of a flower, and the greater order that allows all of life to flourish. It is also seen in many of the events that shape your lives: the birth of a baby, the helping hand, the inventive idea, the creative impulse, the food on your table and every action it took to put it there. Grace is visible everywhere. Grace upholds life on this planet and throughout the universe because life is sacred.

So, now we come to the second teaching: *Acknowledge the hand of Grace in your life.* To connect with your Source and the goodness and love at your core, it is necessary to notice and acknowledge that the Divine is immanent and operative in your life and in every life. If you do not see the truth of this, you will accept your mind's conclusions about life. These conclusions will not serve you, because they are half-truths that leave out the most essential truth—that you are deeply loved and guided in every moment by that which created you and lives in you and through you.

You see, you are never separate from that which created you but, rather, you *are* that which created you. Just as a child is made from the DNA and physical material of the parents, you are made from and of the same love that is the motivating force within the Divine and all of creation. The life force and love that run you run everything, for they are the very essence of God.

But herein lies the rub: You have been given free will, and that allows you to follow the most primitive aspect of yourself—the ego—if you choose. The ego carries and reflects the destructive side of human nature: greed, hatred, selfishness, envy, and jealousy. The ego is driven by fear and a sense of scarcity. It is responsible for perceptions that run counter to your higher nature and to the truth about life. The ego is the cause of all harm and suffering and what makes being human so difficult. And yet, the fear, greed, and hatred of the ego is not your true nature, even though it often succeeds at overshadowing the love that is.

When people are not in touch with the love at their core, they are left with the ego, and they act out its fear, hatred, and greed. This makes it difficult for others around them to be in touch with the love at their core, and so the ego is strengthened in them as well. This is how evil is perpetuated on the planet. Selfishness, hatred, and violence breed more of the same.

What is to break this truly vicious cycle? Only love has the power to break it, for it cannot be broken by more hatred and violence. Who will stop and change the course of history by changing how they behave, even in the face of violence? Unless someone does, then the hatred and violence cannot end.

You must learn to meet hatred and violence with love. This is not a love that accepts abuse, but one that stands up to it and says, "No more will this continue. I refuse to participate in this." If there were no more people willing to fight the wars, the wars would end. This is not to blame the soldiers, because they have been trained to do what they do. But this training and the fear behind it must be examined. The false gives rise only to more of the same: Fear gives rise to more fear, and violence to more violence. Actions based on fear cannot bring peace. Such actions cannot end the wars that rage on earth and in the hearts of humankind.

The only way to end war is to give love to those who hate or fear you. That love might be in the form of food or other provisions that they need. How do you make peace with others? You break bread with them: You sit at their table, eat with them, share your food, laugh with them, and come to know them. This is how peace will come to planet earth, just as peace happens between individuals—through sharing and through kindness.

When I say acknowledge the hand of Grace, I mean become aware of Grace's movement in your life and, once aware, be grateful for it. Gratitude opens your heart to the love and bounty that is continually bestowed upon you. By becoming aware of this bounty and expressing gratitude for it, you counteract the tendency to feel afraid and solitary, abandoned by God, for this is the perception of the ego, especially of those who have met with any abuse in their lives. To allow yourself to be cut off from God in this way is hell. This separation from your Source and from your divine nature is hell.

Of course, you are never truly separate. That would be impossible. But your beliefs are very powerful, and if you believe that you are cut off and if you believe that God has abandoned you or that God is absent from life, then that will be your experience. Unless you open to another possibility, the forces that support life will allow you to have that experience, because you have chosen it. In this way, life is beneficent as well: It allows you to have the experience you choose by believing what you choose to believe until you choose to believe differently and then have a different experience.

Looking for what is good and wondrous about life will bring you to a place of gratitude and connection with the Divine within you and all around you. Choosing to notice the hand of Grace within life and being grateful for it results in an experience of fullness and completeness, which can never be found in the things the ego desires. The life you are given in this magnificent world is all you need to be happy. What an amazing thing it is to be alive in a body, to breathe the air, walk among the hills, drink in the sun, and gaze into another's eyes and see yourself looking back.

You created this world and this life for yourself and for all the other selves to experience. And now you get to choose how you will experience it. How will you meet the challenges of life? With anger or with love? With resentment or gratitude? And how will you meet your failings and the failings of others? With anger or love? With resentment or forgiveness?

In each and every moment you get to choose how you will meet life.

This challenge is made more difficult because you were given an ego, which automatically chooses anger and resentment over love and forgiveness. Will you give that aspect of your humanness your attention? Will you believe the lies the ego tells you? Or will you notice the quiet, gentle peace within that says yes to all difficulties and human failings and chooses to meet them with love and strength, with good will rather than unkindness or negativity?

The ego is a great challenge to human beings, but it is also how you come to know and appreciate your true nature—through such a foil. How interesting it is that you were created to have this duality within you, that you have such a compelling and convincing voice, which takes you away from your own true nature, just so that you can discover and know your true nature more clearly.

You may be wondering where this hand of Grace is. You may think that you do not see it. The answer is that everywhere you look, there it is. Everything has been perfectly designed for your evolution and for awakening to the truth of your divine nature. Every choice you have ever made is exactly the choice you needed to make at the time for you to evolve. And every mistake you have ever made is exactly the mistake you needed to make at the time for you to evolve.

Everyone's journey returns them to the same place: Home. You get to choose the route and how quickly or slowly you travel. That ability to choose is Grace as well. Your life has been designed perfectly to bring you exactly to the point that you are right now, which is exactly where you are meant to be. You cannot make a mistake, for all so-called mistakes still take you where Grace intends.

There is no need for guilt or fear or blame or shame. All of these feelings are ways the ego keeps you from your divine self. These feelings have never helped you be a better person; they have only kept you from connecting with the love and peace at your core. The purpose of the ego is to keep you from seeing the truth about yourself and about life, and fear is the ego's primary means of doing this.

Once you see through this strategy and stop believing the fearful thoughts promoted by the ego, you can begin to trust life. Then the beauty and

Grace become very apparent. Removing fear is like removing a dark film from your glasses. Suddenly the vibrancy and color that were there all along but were hidden by the ego's negativity can be seen. Life is good! How could it be anything but that when love is the reigning force? When you realize that only your perceptions and beliefs make life terrible, you will be free from human suffering and on your way to becoming a butterfly.

THE THIRD TEACHING

Declare Your Deepest Desire

What do you really want? This question is an important one because the answer determines where your energy, attention, and resources go. The answer is therefore also likely to determine what you will get. Sometimes you are not even aware of what you want, and other times that is all you are aware of, and you suffer over it.

The problem with desires is that you have a lot of them and many of them seem overly important, even essential to your happiness. The mind has a way of framing a desire as essential and important when it is not. When I say "the mind," I am referring to what some have called "the egoic mind," or the aspect of the mind that appears as thoughts and is reflective of the ego. I am not referring to the rational side of the mind, or intellect, but to a more irrational part of the mind that reflects your conditioning, including desires and beliefs.

Desires that are not really important but seem so are a challenge that is built into the human condition. Without this illusion, you would see your way Home much more quickly. But that is the point of the illusion. You are not meant to go Home quickly but to have a variety of experiences. How better to do this than by going after one desire and then another? Following your desires provides you with opportunities to taste what life has to offer, and that is how it is meant to be.

So, even your more superficial desires are not a mistake; they just are not what they pretend to be. They are not actually important, and they do not bring you the peace and happiness you really want. More often, going after what you want and even getting what you want reap the opposite of peace, either because you suffer over not having what you want, you become disillusioned with what you desired once you get it, or you are afraid someone will take it from you. There is no peaceful resting place in the land of desire, when those desires come from the ego.

The ego is part of the programming designed to create the human experience, including the suffering that belongs to the human experience. Yes, you are programmed to suffer, as this suffering drives life and drives your learning and evolution as a soul. Growth comes about in this earthly dimension largely as a result of wanting to avoid suffering. Eventually you discover the truth about life—what life is about and who you really are—because your suffering leads you to those who have answers to questions that come out of the depths of your suffering.

Having many desires keeps everyone very busy. And yet all of these desires can be reduced to a few deeper ones. For instance, when you want a new car, what do you really want? Love? Admiration? Belonging? If you already felt loved, admired, and part of something greater, would you still want a new car? Maybe. But if you already felt loved, admired, and part of something greater, then getting a new car would have less meaning. It wouldn't be weighted with the heavy responsibility of providing you with love, admiration, and belonging, which is asking too much of a car. The car's responsibility would be appropriate to the car: You would want it to take you places effectively, comfortably, and safely, which is something a car can potentially do. And why do you want love, admiration, and belonging? What would these give you? Wouldn't they just allow you to rest and be at peace? Isn't that what you really want?

The same is true of other things that you want. Many want a relationship because they imagine that it will make them blissfully happy. Yet, that is asking too much of a relationship. It can give you companionship, but your happiness is something only you can give yourself. People expect too much from the things they want. Most things people want can give them only a fraction of what they want. The deeper things, such as happiness, peace, and love, do not come from material things or accomplishments but are a state of mind, or more accurately, a state of heart. The deeper things come from a way of being *in* life. They are *how* you are in life and have nothing to do with what you have, where you live, or who you think you are.

How do you achieve this state of happiness and peace, this state of *being*, that you really long for? There is only one way, and that is to unmask the illusion, the mistaken belief, that peace and happiness are not here and that you have to do something to get them. You do not have to get or do something to be happy and at peace, as the mind presumes. The secret is to stop trying to get or do something to be happy and at peace.

The secret is to just stop and be. Just stop and be in this moment, without all of the ideas and desires about who you want to be or how you want life to be (in the future). What is true right here and now? What is your experience right here and now? Breathing in and breathing out is happening. What else are you aware of? Is there peace in this simple moment? Happiness? Love? Yes they are all here now.

But that is too easy—and boring—to the mind. Do you listen to the mind? Do you let the mind take you away from this simple moment? Breathing in and breathing out. Simplicity itself. Just this. Just being right here and now in this moment. That is what being alive in this moment is like. No person having to chase rainbows. Just rainbows here, now. Delight in life just as it is. This is the freedom and love you have always wanted, that you have been looking for all of your life. You are the love and peace you have been looking for. You are made of love and peace. Why go looking for it? It is here, right now in the stillness of just being.

In the moments when you are not experiencing love and peace, declare your desire for them. This cannot be an empty declaration of words only, however. With this declaration, this intention, you must also turn your attention away from what distracts you from the peace and love that are already here. You must turn your attention away from the lies your mind tells you about life and what it thinks you need to be happy.

Your declaration must be followed by an effort— yes, a choice—to shift your attention. It is not difficult to do this. It is not hard work but the simplest thing imaginable. How hard is it to move your attention from one thing to another? A million times a day you do this, so how hard can it be? To experience the peace and love that you most desire requires only that you shift your attention from your ideas about yourself and what you think you need to be happy to the here and now. And then keep your attention there. If your attention drifts away again into thought, then shift your attention once again to here and now.

You can bring your attention to your breath, as many who meditate do, or simply to a sensation you are having, and that will anchor you in your body, which is the mechanism for experiencing real life. The mind is the mechanism for experiencing a subjective, internal, and to a large extent made-up reality, while the body registers actual reality. How peaceful it is to be in reality without the subjective overlay of the mind! Peace at last. Is it enough? It is not enough for the mind, but is it enough for *you*?

You are not your mind, are you? Your mind carries on, and sometimes you are lost in it and sometimes not. Aren't you what is lost or not lost in the mind? Aren't you what is conscious of being lost or not being lost? What a strange mystery you are. Does this consciousness have a personality? A gender? Preferences? A particular style or appearance? No, it just moves, in and out of thought, in and out of being the character you appear to be, in and out of various roles and identities you play. But you are not any of these things. You are the consciousness that moves in and out of these things.

Where is the peace in all of this? Is it not in the moments when you are outside identification with the character's mind and desires and its ideas about itself and its life? Is there peace in the mind, desires, roles, or identities? Isn't peace outside such things? Doesn't it come when you are aware of yourself beyond these things?

What is this mysterious thing you call yourself, which is beyond thought, beyond feelings, beyond roles, personas, and self-images? Who you are is nothing you can put your finger on, is it? It is nothing you can define or describe. The mind draws a blank in the face of it, so the mind turns away and thinks about something it can describe or define, something words are suited for.

What do you really want? Are you ready to declare that? Are you ready to give peace and love your attention? Are you ready to choose peace and love instead of some fleeting desire churned out by the ego? This may not seem like an important question, but it is extremely important, because it marks a turning point in one's evolution, when it becomes possible to finally get what you really want. Are you willing to turn away from, or at least not give so much importance to, your other desires? You might not be, and that's fine too. But if you are ready, then declare your deepest desire. This is my third teaching. *Declare that you want peace and love.* Feel the depth and power of this desire and let it fuel your will to give peace and love your attention.

You and the spiritual forces that support your evolution will jointly bring peace and love into your life when you declare that you want these things more than anything else. Everyone's evolution eventually comes to this: You realize that your deepest desire is for peace and love and you declare this in your heart. Then life conspires to bring you exactly that. Are you ready to know the truth about life and the truth about yourself—that you are what you desire most deeply? You are love and peace. Your life has always been about discovering this.

THE FOURTH TEACHING

Accept Life as It Is

It is impossible to love or feel at peace unless you accept life as it is. Non-acceptance closes the heart, which is the doorway to love and peace. There is no other way but acceptance to open that door. When you accept, peace comes and love can flow once again.

This is a hard truth for the mind to swallow, because the mind is designed to reject, resist, and desire something other than the way life is. The mind does not accept the way things are: It does not accept cold when it wants warmth or rain when it wants sunshine. It can even be upset over vanilla ice cream when it wants chocolate instead. The mind believes that life should go according to its ideas and plans. And like a willful child, it complains and is angered when life does not. Listening to the mind ensures that the heart will stay closed. If you take the mind's perspective as yours, then you will be at odds with life, you will not find happiness, and you will not experience lasting peace or love.

This resistance is natural and how you were built to respond to life. Nevertheless, there is another way. You do not have to let your mind determine your inner experience. You do not have to be upset by what the mind is upset about. The mind's rejection of the way life is does not have to be your internal experience—your experience of life. There is another possibility. Do you want love and peace more than you want what the mind wants? (This should be easy to answer when you realize that the mind does not get what it wants anyway just because it wants it.) Are you willing to see that you are not the mind?

Is the mind wise enough to know what is best for it? Like a child, the mind does not know, but it thinks it knows. Fortunately, you are inherently wise. Although you have a mind that often refuses to see the truth, something else within you knows the truth. Unlike the child, you actually know that you cannot have life as you want it, that life is what it is and it will be what it will be. The mind thinks it can change this, but it cannot. The mind will be forever unhappy as long as it believes that life can be changed in ways that it cannot be changed. The child that is the mind does not grow up. It continues to believe its erroneous beliefs in spite of evidence to the contrary. It does not learn. It does not grow. But you are already grown up and see the truth. You are not the mind.

Look to that which is wise within you to determine your stance toward life. Your internal experience is governed either by you or by your mind. Your subjective experience is in your control, while much of life is not. Take the reins back from the mind. Take control of your subjective experience. Align your perspective with the truth about life, and do not allow the mind to tell you how to think or feel.

Peace and love can be how you feel about life rather than resistance and unhappiness, anger and discord. Find that which is within you that loves and is at peace with life just as it is. *That* has always been awake and aware within you. It is the only thing that has ever been awake and aware, but it gets overlooked in the jumble of thoughts that occupy your attention. Take back your power, which you have given to the mind, to determine your experience of life.

Accepting the realities of life includes accepting your own pain and limitations as a human being. You have a human body, with all the pain and limitations of that. You have false ideas, which create painful emotions. You have tendencies that also cause suffering, such as judging, wanting to be superior, and comparing yourself with others. This is all as it is meant to be. There are no mistakes here. You are designed this way, and this must be accepted. But fortunately, you are also given the capability of overcoming the suffering and limitations of the human condition.

What powerful creators you are! With just your thoughts, you create feelings. These feelings propel you to behave in often destructive ways, which reap certain consequences and more feelings. Then those feelings are acted on, and on it goes. This is the human experience. When you see how this works, it becomes possible to accept the way things are within the human experience and move beyond such human tendencies. If you do not see how this works, you are at the mercy of your humanness, and accepting the seemingly endless suffering caused by your thoughts and feelings will be difficult.

Acceptance of life and of the human condition requires awareness of the truth about life and the human condition, because it is very difficult, if not impossible, to accept what you are unaware of. If you are unaware of the truth, how can you accept it? You will continue to adhere to the perspective you were given—the mind's perspective, which is false.

Becoming aware of the truth about life and the human condition is key to being at peace and to becoming the loving being that you can be. Once you are aware of the human dilemma, of why being human is so difficult, then you are no longer at the mercy of the human condition, and it is possible to experience yourself very differently. Once you experience that you are the loving being that you have always wanted to be, and not the mind, then it is easy to love and accept your human self and to love and accept those who are still caught in the human condition—because you understand their dilemma.

The challenge in escaping the self-loathing and lack that you experience as a human is accepting yourself when you feel this way about yourself. At some point, you realize that acceptance is the key to unlocking the prison of the human condition. Perhaps you hear it from a wise soul or run across it in a book. The keys to the prison are out there when you are ready to find them. I offer this key to you as the most important teaching of all, my fourth teaching: *Accept life as it is and accept yourself as you are.*

How is this done? What is the mechanism of acceptance? If you look closely at those moments when you are in acceptance, what is it that you do or do not do that allows you to accept something? Doesn't acceptance come more from *not* doing something than from doing something? Doesn't acceptance happen when you *stop* arguing that you or he or she or life should be different, when you give up the fight against the way things are? You surrender to things just the way they are, including surrendering your resistance to the way things are.

You let your resistance, your rejection, your anger, your frustration with the way life is to just be there.

Then you *do* something. What you do is recognize that the resistance, rejection, anger, frustration, and anything else you are feeling do not belong to you. That's right—they do not belong to you but to the human condition. Your feelings belong to humanity; they are part of your humanity. And you sit with these feelings, with compassion for the pain they cause you and all of humanity. You recognize your feelings for what they are: a byproduct of the human condition. In that moment you are free, no longer at the mercy of them.

This freedom is the experience of your true nature. You have always been this free, but you have been playing at being human. You have been moving in and out of the human experience, but all along you have never been human. You have always been both that which is aware of being human and that which experiences being human. What a paradox: You are both human and not human!

When you become aware of who you truly are, then being human becomes so much easier. Being human is no longer a problem, because you have accepted your humanity, and that acceptance enables you to be free from the suffering caused by being human and free to be who you really are. This is why acceptance is the most powerful teaching of all: It is the key to freeing yourself from the human condition. This key is given to you when it is time to step out of the prison, and no sooner. Everything has been designed to bring you to this moment of awakening.

Acceptance has a potential pitfall: Accepting your humanness and feelings does not mean indulging them. This can be a fine line to walk. Walking this razor's edge takes practice. After accepting the human condition, rather than returning to your humanness and letting your feelings play themselves out in the usual ways, the next step is to give your attention to the life you are given in this moment, not the life the mind dreams of, but life as it is showing up in the here and now.

Once you become aware of the mind's role in creating the human condition and you accept that the mind does what it does and perceives as it perceives, then you must *choose* to give your attention to something other than the mind. If you give your attention to the mind, you will perpetuate the human conditioning that you have received rather than move beyond it. It is your choice. Awareness and acceptance make this choice possible.

THE FIFTH TEACHING

Realize That Your Thoughts and Feelings Are Not Yours

What if your thoughts and feelings were not yours? What if by some odd occurrence, your thoughts and feelings were exchanged with someone else's? Would you still be who you are? This is a profound question and worth pondering. If you answered yes, what is it that remains if your thoughts and feelings were no longer the same? How much would this change your behavior and how you see yourself? Would you suddenly behave and see yourself differently?

The extent to which you tend to identify with, believe, and act out your thoughts and feelings is the extent to which this thought and feeling exchange would matter. Or would it? How different are your thoughts and feelings from other people's? Don't all people have similar thoughts and feelings? Aren't you essentially more like other human beings than different from them? Do your thoughts and feelings make you unique, or does something else make you unique?

Your needs, drives, and desires are similar to every other human being's. You may have different preferences and a different personality style, but these differences do not make you different from other human beings in a fundamental way. Everyone has the same needs, drives, and desires: for survival, food, water, sleep, shelter, security, safety, comfort, love, belonging, happiness, peace, and beauty. These are some of the basic drives that unite all human beings.

All human beings also have similar feelings: Everyone feels fear, joy, love, guilt, anger, shame, jealousy, envy, hatred, and greed. Only the extent to which these feelings are acted on varies, but they exist in all human beings. An argument could be made that some people, namely sociopaths, lack feelings of guilt and shame. However, those individuals are universally acknowledged as aberrant.

Because all humans have similar drives, needs, desires, and feelings, it is easy enough to conclude that their thoughts are similar as well, since thoughts go hand-in-hand with drives, needs, desires, and feelings. So, even without knowing exactly what everyone else is thinking, it is safe to assume that people have very similar thoughts going through their minds.

So, generally speaking, what makes people different is the extent to which they believe and act on their thoughts and which thoughts they believe and act on. For instance, someone who is successful most likely disregards thoughts that might interfere with success and embraces those that support success, while someone who is less successful most likely does the opposite. Although nothing, including success, is completely dependent on one's thoughts, your relationship to your thoughts really matters.

The same is true of feelings: Your relationship to your feelings, particularly to uncomfortable feelings, really matters. Your relationship to your feelings determines whether you will feel bad or not and how you will behave. The feelings that you believe and focus on are strengthened and become determining forces in your life, while ones you brush off have little effect at all.

Relating to difficult feelings in a way that does not aggravate them or cause them to be a problem in your life is a skill that must be learned. It takes some effort to become conscious of your thoughts and feelings. Most people are not aware of what they are thinking and feeling, nor do they realize that they have a choice about how they will respond to their thoughts and feelings. Most people react to their thoughts and feelings without realizing that there is another way to relate to them that is likely to be less problematic.

This lack of awareness causes people to be victims of their own humanness, of the thoughts they were given. The human condition is a state of suffering for the simple reason that people do not naturally question their thoughts and feelings. They assume that their thoughts are valid, and they assume that their thoughts are *their* thoughts. These are mistaken assumptions that lead to so much pain.

These assumptions are at the root of human suffering.

So again, what if your thoughts and feelings were not yours? They are what give you the experience of being a human being, while you are actually much more than a human being: You are a spiritual being. So, when I say that your thoughts and feelings are not yours, I mean that they have nothing to do with the spiritual being that you are and everything to do with the human being that you actually are not. There is nothing wrong with being a human being, of course, except that identifying with what makes you human—your thoughts and feelings—means that you will suffer.

There is a time in your evolution when suffering is meant to be the driving force. Suffering carries evolution forward. And there comes a time when suffering is no longer necessary and the evolutionary lesson is how *not* to suffer within the human condition, because this is possible. You could say that how not to suffer while being human is the last lesson before graduating to a more divine state. Many are ready to learn how to do this, and many are teaching this, because humanity is reaching a critical point in its evolution, where human beings must learn to live in greater harmony and peace.

Suffering is caused by the resistance, sense of lack, and false beliefs of the egoic mind. Attaining peace and happiness is largely a matter of moving beyond such thoughts and beliefs. You move beyond them simply by not believing them. The pain that results from believing such thoughts drives the discovery of this truth. You eventually see that these thoughts are not true and not helpful, that they have betrayed and misled you.

What is it that is capable of seeing this great truth? You are! When you connect with your divine nature, you feel wise, peaceful, and loving. When you believe your thoughts, you feel lacking, fearful, and unloving and you lose touch with the truth about yourself and about life. Your thoughts create a sense of being someone who struggles with life. Without these thoughts, you are free to experience life as the beautiful and joy-filled gift that it is.

To return to our inquiry, if your thoughts and feelings are not yours, then do they matter? They seemed to matter because, after all, they were *yours*. Aren't they what make you *you*? Who are you if you are not these thoughts? They are what make up the human you, but they are not what make up the real you. They shroud the real you, in fact. What a surprise to discover this. Who are you, really? Aren't you what is able to see this truth? Aren't you what is beyond all thoughts and feelings? So, again, do your thoughts and feelings matter? What if they do not? Then what? On what basis do you live life if not on the basis of your thoughts and feelings?

This teaching, that *your thoughts and feelings are not yours*, is the fifth teaching. It is a teaching upon which all else turns. Your life as you knew it ends the moment you accept this teaching, and a new life can begin, as you try out your butterfly wings and discover that, yes, there is a new way to live that does not include suffering. All you had to do was turn away from the egoic mind and be here in this beautiful life just as it is. But how do you do that? This brings us to the sixth teaching...

THE SIXTH TEACHING

Be with What Is Real

What remains when thoughts and feelings are no longer believed, when they no longer matter? You are still here, right? Nothing really changed, and yet everything changed, because your relationship to life changed. Before, your thoughts and feelings were seen as primary and important; now, they fall into the background, and the rest of life becomes the foreground. As with the optical illusions you have all enjoyed, where the foreground suddenly becomes background, everything looks different, and yet nothing actually changed, only your perception. When the lenses of perception are no longer clouded by thoughts and feelings related to your human self, then it becomes obvious who the looker, the real witness of life, is and what is false and what is real.

The problem with thoughts and feelings is that they do not accurately reflect reality, and often they have no connection whatsoever with reality, although they pretend to. In a sense, thoughts and feelings create a parallel reality, one that contains the *you* that you think of yourself as, although that is all that that *you* is. It is just ideas about you, mostly images and stories. This parallel reality exists only in your own mind (not even in other people's minds). It is a made-up reality that shapes and determines your experience of reality to the extent that you believe this imagined reality.

For example, if you believe you are unattractive, then you feel unattractive and you are likely to spend a good deal of your time trying to change your appearance in an attempt to fix how you feel about yourself. Some of the things you do might be felt to help temporarily. But you cannot really fix an idea about yourself by changing something on the outside. You can only change an idea about yourself by changing your relationship to that idea. The problem is not that you are unattractive but that you *believe* you are unattractive.

All of your efforts to change your appearance and your feelings about it would be unnecessary if you didn't believe the thought that you are not attractive or if that thought didn't matter to you. Then what would you do with your time and energy? If spending time trying to be better looking were fulfilling, then doing this wouldn't be a problem. However, not feeling good about yourself and then spending time trying to fix that, which cannot be fixed on the outside anyway, is not fulfilling. Doing these things does not bring joy or peace, only the opposite. So, what is the point in doing them? They can never truly satisfy, and that is the problem with believing the mind. It presents you with problems that are false issues and solutions to those problems that will never satisfy.

Life does not have to be spent in such ways. It can be spent in more fulfilling and joyful ways, but how will you find out what is possible if you are busy trying to fix imaginary problems and the feelings that stem from them?

What if thoughts and feelings do not matter? Within the human condition, thoughts and feelings matter so much—so much that people are willing to die and kill for them. Giving so much weight to thoughts and feelings is responsible for the suffering on this planet. What I am suggesting is moving beyond the human condition and the suffering by moving beyond thoughts and feelings. I am talking about a way of being that is as different from the usual way of being as a butterfly is from a caterpillar.

The next phase in humanity's evolution is a phase in which thoughts and feelings are seen for what they are and so they do not matter. They are disregarded. I am not talking about repressing feelings, as often happens within the human condition, but not creating feelings in the first place by not believing the thoughts that cause them. If the thoughts are not believed, then the feelings are not experienced. And if feelings *are* experienced, they are seen for what they are: reflections of a mistaken idea, one that was taken seriously when it should not have been.

Imagine, for a moment, what it would be like if someone who was angry at you disregarded that anger or if you disregarded your anger. How would that change your relationships? What can disturb the natural state of peace that the evolved human is capable of? Only a thought can ever disturb that peace. Only a thought—only something as insubstantial as a thought can bring war and terror into human interactions. Once you become a butterfly, you see the absurdity of giving so much power to thoughts and feelings. There have always been ones who walked the planet who saw the absurdity of this. They were and are your spiritual teachers and the masters who founded the various religions. They all taught peace.

What has happened to this teaching of peace? It has been corrupted by the mind, which claims that peace is impossible—and worse!—unsafe. This is the big lie that keeps people stuck in the suffering of the human condition. Peace is possible, and it is even possible right now in your world. But it starts with you—within your own heart, and then spreads to others.

How can you know the truth or trust it if you haven't discovered it for yourself by living as if your thoughts and feelings do not matter? Will you give your thoughts and feelings power by believing them, or will you disengage from them and discover "the peace that passeth all understanding"? Only then will you know peace.

Once you learn to disengage from your thoughts and feelings, all that is left is to *be with what is real.* This is the sixth teaching and the basis for a new life as a butterfly, a newly awakened human being. Once the false and unreal, or illusory, is disregarded, all that is left is what is real.

What *is* real? Look around. What do you see and touch and feel and smell and taste? That is real. What you experience through your senses is as real as it gets. Without your senses, there is no world to experience, although consciousness still exists. So, consciousness is also real. These things: sensory experience and consciousness make up the world of the butterfly.

Yes, thoughts and feelings exist within experience, but they are understood to be what upholds the illusion of a suffering self, struggling against life. Sensory experience and consciousness cannot produce suffering, only joy. So, when your focus is on sensory experience and consciousness, suffering is impossible. Without suffering, the joy, peace, and love of your true nature shine through, because they are no longer obscured by the reality made up by thought. Thoughts and feelings have become background, while sensory experience and consciousness have become foreground. This new way of being and perceiving is marked by joy, peace, and a sense of having come Home.

For our purposes, I'd like to define anything that takes you away from what is real as *unreal* and anything that comes from what is real or brings you more in touch with what is real as *real*. Given this, the products of the mind—thoughts and feelings—are unreal; while joy, peace, love, courage, patience, fortitude, wisdom, intuition, inspiration, and some types of motivation are real.

Be with what is real means give your attention to what is real. Whatever you give your attention to becomes real to you. So, if you give your attention to what is unreal—thoughts and feelings—then these will seem real: They become your reality. On the other hand, if you give your attention to sensory experience and consciousness, then what is real becomes your reality. You become aligned with the truth about life rather than caught in illusion.

It is obvious enough what it means to give your attention to sensory experience. But what does it mean to give your attention to consciousness? And who is it that can choose to give attention to consciousness instead of something else? That can only be consciousness, since consciousness is the only thing that exists. Everything is consciousness. Everything is made of the same thing. In this game of life, after being lost in the illusion spun by the mind, one fine day, consciousness becomes aware of itself as consciousness. It wakes up to the truth.

Language falls short in describing the truth about who you are. I am using *consciousness* to refer to what is conscious and aware. This consciousness is the great mystery: What is conscious and aware? Whatever this is does not have a color, a gender, a personality, preferences, or even a body. It is not even a *what* or a *who*, because it is not a thing that is separate from other things. Rather it is all things. Consciousness is who you are and who everyone else and everything else is.

It is easy to experience consciousness. You cannot *not* experience it. Consciousness is what allows you to be conscious and aware of your existence. So, when I say turn your attention to consciousness, I simply mean become aware that you are aware. Notice what is conscious and aware. Notice what notices. Turn the spotlight of your attention onto attention itself. What is it that is aware and conscious of existing? Notice this. This is what is real.

What happens when you turn awareness in on itself is that the sense of who you are gets stronger. You experience who you are more strongly. So, becoming aware of awareness is critical in overcoming the human condition. The more you become aware of who you really are, the easier it is to see who you are *not*, and you will cease being fooled by the egoic mind.

You are experiencing consciousness through the sensing mechanism that is your body, so consciousness may seem to be located within your body. When you say, "I am conscious," it really feels like you exist inside your skin. However, if you examine this more closely, you will discover that it only seems this way, that consciousness is both inside and outside of your body and has no boundary whatsoever. And yet, it seems like *your* consciousness, your awareness.

This is confusing to the mind, and the mind will never understand this. But there are many things the mind will never understand. This paradox—that you are both an individual and not an individual is at the heart of the great mystery of being. You are manifesting as an individual *and* as that which is beyond this individual, and so is everyone else. What is beyond you and beyond others is, of course, the same. There is actually only one consciousness manifesting in a multitude of ways, in everything that exists. Only one.

This great truth is the teaching known as *nonduality*, which means "not two." Oneness is the truth behind all of existence, which is acknowledged by every mystic and religion. This truth is undeniable, except by the mind, which cannot comprehend this and does not want to see the truth. Everything in this universe is a manifestation of the same thing. When two people or two nations fight, Oneness is at play on both sides, playing the various roles necessary for conflict. Does Oneness, therefore, like conflict? Conflict is one way that Oneness is exploring life—through two-ness and through two people or nations hating or loving each other.

Oneness wishes to have every possible experience, even conflict, so it creates worlds wherein it can have these experiences. Oneness loves to create, so it manifests all manner of things and experiences. You are extensions of the Creator, which allow it to create and experience within this physical world. And when you shed your personhood, your physical body, you continue to exist and create in other dimensions.

Everyone and everything is inseparable from Oneness. It is you, and you are it, just as surely as wetness is inseparable from water. So, when you see something, consciousness sees it. When you experience something, consciousness experiences it. This is how it is meant to be. When you give your attention to thoughts and feelings, you have a human experience; when you do not do that, you have an experience of pure consciousness as it lives through your body.

Once you have awakened from the human condition, you remain for a time within a human body while knowing yourself as consciousness, free of the limiting illusions of the mind. This is what a master is: someone who lives as consciousness while walking on this earth. He or she is "in the world but not of it." He or she has become a butterfly. This is the future of all of humanity.

When you give your attention to consciousness, you are merging your attention with its source. Your attention is no longer coopted by the mind. Your awareness is pure, no longer clouded by illusion. Therefore, your awareness can experience life purely, without the influence of the mind.

Consciousness's experience of life is that of joy, awe, wonder, love, and peace. When you are filled with gratitude for the gift that life is, you are experiencing what pure consciousness naturally experiences. Life untarnished by the mind and purely experienced is exquisite. This is the reward for discovering the truth. It is the great treasure that is meant to be found by each and every one of you.

By being with what is real, you get a taste of this pure consciousness. The longer you are able to stay with what is real, which is a matter of being very present to life, the more familiar you become with the Oneness at your core, and the more it begins to live your life.

You give your attention to what is real because what is real is the ultimate reward, although it can take a long time to realize that what you have been looking for lies in this direction instead of in the directions that your mind points you toward. When you are done looking everywhere else, you finally become willing to look right here and now at what is real and true in front of you, and then you find it: the peace that you always knew in your heart was possible.

THE SEVENTH TEACHING

Follow Your Joy

You were given a compass, and that compass is joy.
You are meant to go in the direction that brings joy,
not in the direction that brings suffering. The egoic
mind promises you joy but delivers only temporary
satisfaction and happiness. Then the suffering that
comes with feeling that you never have enough
returns.

Most people do not follow their joy. Instead,
they follow the sense of not having or being enough.
They allow the sense of lack to drive them forward,
seeking here and there for fulfillment, for what will
fill the sense of lack created by the human condition,
the ego.

However, nothing that the egoic mind suggests can fill that lack, because the sense of lack was created by the same thing that proposes to fix it. How can something (the ego) that creates a sense of lack also solve the problem of feeling lacking—and why would it? The solution cannot be found by chasing after the ideas presented by the very thing that created the problem. The sense of lack cannot be solved by the egoic mind, no matter how convincing the egoic mind sounds.

The sense of lack can only be solved by dropping out of the mind. When you drop out of the mind, you lose the sense that anything is lacking. That is an easy solution! There never was anything lacking, and that is all you have ever had to see to feel full and complete. Nothing was ever needed except to see the truth: Nothing is lacking in you, in others, or in life.

The sense of lack is part of the illusion created by the mind. When you know you are not your mind, then the illusion of lack disappears—no more lack! Nothing is or ever was lacking. The belief that something is lacking makes this seem true, but it is not true. Your beliefs are powerful! You create the experience of lack simply by believing that something is lacking.

The sense of lack is so ingrained that most people are unaware that it is there. They just react to it as if it were true. For most, the sense of lack is a deeply held belief. It seems absolutely and unquestionably true: "Of course I'm lacking. Of course my life is lacking! And I have to do something about it or I'll never be happy."

This is the lie that keeps the illusion going. So, off you go trying to fix yourself and your life, when the problem is that you are focused on a sense of self and a sense of lack that is not actually real. The truth is that there is nothing to fix about yourself and your life. All is well just as it is. There is no problem with you or with life being just as it is.

The sense of yourself and the sense of lack are both manufactured by the mind. They create the human condition that is one of suffering. You not only believe you are who you *think* you are, but these thoughts about yourself tell you that you are lacking and that your life—indeed, life itself—is not good enough.

This unrelenting sense of lack interferes with the joy that is possible whenever you are willing to simply be with whatever is showing up in your life. This sense of lack becomes a state of consciousness that you live in without realizing that you are living in it. Like a fish in water, you do not even know you are living under the spell of an illusion, the false idea that you need to do or be something different to be okay and to be happy. This assumption causes you to overlook the happiness that is present at your core and ever available in this simple and sweet present moment.

The happiness at your core is very subtle unless you turn your attention to it and allow yourself to experience it for more than a brief second. What usually happens instead is that the ego's sense of lack overshadows this subtle happiness and compels you to think or do something to try to feel better. When your attention is focused on fixing a perceived problem, it is not available to notice the quiet beauty, peace, and joy that are already present within you.

The subtle happiness of your true nature is experienced only when you are present in the here and now. To the ego, it seems like nothing much is going on in the here and now. The ego likes drama, action, and feeling special. If those things are not happening, then the ego is not interested in the here and now, and it would rather daydream, fantasize, plan, or create a problem than experience the peace of life happening as it happens most of the time.

When you are identified with the egoic mind, you are not interested in being present, because being present seems boring and pointless. If this were not the case, people could be happy much more easily. But this little lie—that being present is boring and pointless—keeps people entranced by the mind and believing its other lies, all of which tell you that there is no other way to live than how you are living. As long as you believe that being present to life is not worthwhile, you will not find out that you are meant to live in a very different way. The unmasking of this lie is the key to happiness and the key to peace on earth. But each person has to find this out for himself or herself. And everyone eventually does.

The story of human existence has a happy ending. Eventually everyone discovers the truth about the human condition and how to move beyond suffering. Everyone eventually becomes a master. The keys are right here in this little book and in simply being present.

I am offering these teachings now because peace must come to earth. You must come together as one people, or this world might not continue to support human life. You must come together to solve your problems, and you must come together so that you do not destroy each other and the natural world. This teaching of peace is not only for your personal well-being but, more importantly, so that humankind may become more peaceful. It is time to see through the illusion and lies spun by the egoic mind. It is time for many of you to become butterflies.

Speaking metaphorically again, the difference between a caterpillar and a butterfly is what moves them. Caterpillars are moved by fear and a sense of lack, while butterflies are moved by joy. These are two very different ways of being.

The caterpillar's life is a prison of sorts, in which one's life is created by reacting to fear and lack. The caterpillar does not know its own potential as a butterfly nor does it realize that it is in prison. The caterpillar cannot imagine what is possible, and it is afraid to. It does not trust life. It does not know that life is a gift that was given for the purpose of learning, growing, playing, and creating. Similarly, most people do not know their own potential, as they allow themselves to be defined by the fears and mistaken beliefs of the mind.

The Source creates through you with joy. It moves and inspires you with joy. In joy, you are free to explore all possibilities. You are free to move beyond limitations of thought, free to experience yourself *as* joy, which you are! Knowing this joy and following it is the only difference between a caterpillar and a butterfly. But it is a big difference.

Joy is native and natural to you. It is in your heart and always has been. Everyone knows joy, but the mind often says things that cause you to deny joy or move in ways opposed to it. Joy is enthusiasm and gratitude for life. It bursts forth to be expressed in the world as creativity and love. Along with love, joy is the motivating force in the universe. It is not separate from love, although language makes it seem so. Joy and love are part of the same force, and this force is the consciousness behind all life. How could being true to it possibly lead you astray?

The mind's perspective is that love and joy are nice, but they are not safe, not as safe as fear. The mind tells you that your fears are important and you need them to be safe. This is a lie. Fearful thoughts only keep you chained to caterpillar consciousness. Indeed, that is their purpose, for your divine nature does not guide and protect you with such thoughts. Your divine nature does not need thoughts at all to move and inspire you. Joy is not a thought; it is a force, a feeling that propels you forward to fulfill your destiny.

Yes, each of you has a destiny. You are part of a grand design. Your place and destiny are revealed by joy. Joy is the guiding force in butterfly consciousness. You are meant to be a butterfly, and joy is how you become one. Find the joy within you— that *is* you! Then go where that joy wants to go, do what that joy wants to do, and say what that joy wants to say. Being a butterfly is as simple as that. The mind wants to complicate this with "what ifs," but there is never a good reason to not follow your joy. Is that unbelievable? You may think so. Is it really that simple? Yes. This is my seventh teaching: *Follow your joy.* Now onto the how...

THE EIGHTH TEACHING

Be Still

Unless you become still, you may not know your joy, which does not arise from the mind but from beyond it. Unless you move beyond your mind, you will experience the joy at your core only very briefly and faintly. To experience this joy requires making space for it—empty space, free from thought. In this space, it is possible—indeed, probable—that you will experience who you really are.

In between each and every thought is a space, and that is where freedom lies, in experiencing this space. How simple it is to experience it! Anyone can do it. And yet, staying in that experience of space can be so hard. Are you able to experience that space and the sense of spaciousness that comes from that for a moment?

What is this space like? Is peace there? Is love there? Are clarity and wisdom there? Is strength there? Courage? Patience? Compassion? Yes, all of the qualities of your divine nature are there. That is where they have always been and where they can always be found again when you need them. All you have to do is give your attention to the space in between thoughts instead of to your thoughts. But that attention must be given for more than a second, or the qualities of your true nature will fade quickly from your awareness, as thoughts and the experience that thought creates take over.

What is the experience of thought like? Does it make you more peaceful, more loving, more courageous, more compassionate? Possibly, but usually not. More likely, thought causes tension, because underlying so much of it is the sense of not being or having enough. Thought so often results in the feeling of having a problem or needing to work harder, strive harder, try harder. Thought causes your energy to move outward. Much of the time, thought drives you to act.

Putting your attention on the space in between thoughts, on the other hand, feels very different. When you do this, you feel spacious, expanded, quiet, content, and receptive to life. And yet, this spaciousness does not make you passive, as wise action naturally flows from it.

In this space, motivation is not lacking; rather, this space is the source of true motivation. Action that comes out of spaciousness is propelled by joy, by a sense of purpose that feels expansive and right, rather than driven by fear or a sense of lack. Action inspired by your depths embraces life joyfully, gratefully, and excitedly.

Once you are convinced that this space has value, you will begin to give it more attention. Nevertheless, the mind will try to pull you out of this state of peace and contentment. To stay for longer periods of time and eventually to live from this space, requires commitment and diligence. The ego's tendency to run from stillness and peace has to be overcome. It runs from the spaciousness because the ego's viability and power depend on you not going into the space, because if you do, you will not be the same.

The *you* that is created by the mind cannot be sustained in this space. It disappears, and what you are left with is a feeling of spaciousness. When the *me* disappears, you become aware of who you really are, which is not a thing and is therefore experienced as nothing, or space. Without thoughts about yourself, there is no egoic self, no false self. What makes this self false is that it is solely created by ideas about yourself—and false ideas at that. When such thoughts stop or are no longer given attention, the false sense of self ceases. Then you are left with space, with the experience of who you really are.

Indeed, you are not a thing, not a body, not a mind, and not a personality but pure consciousness. When thought is no longer controlling your attention, you experience that which is beyond thought and the false self that is created by thought. You experience who you really are.

What you discover is very wonderful! You *are* peace, compassion, love, wisdom, clarity, strength, courage, patience, and every other virtue. You are all that is good. What if it were otherwise? The nightmare you have been living is that you are bad, not good enough, flawed, and incomplete.

Fortunately, none of that is true. This sense of yourself has been manufactured by the egoic mind, and it is false.

When the mind is quiet, you are left with the truth: You are complete goodness and love, like that which created you. This is the happy ending that everyone longs for. The most wonderful discovery possible occurs at the end of your spiritual journey: You realize that you are divine and so is everyone else.

The way to arrive at this destination is to *be still*. Choosing to be still is a powerful choice, for without it, the understanding of who you are will be merely an intellectual one, not a living realization. The only way to realize your true nature is to move out of the intellect and into the experience of your true nature. You do this by being still.

The teaching could just as well be *just be*. This phrase points to a state of being in which there is no subject, no *I*, and no further definition, no adjectives to describe that state of being. How you get to this state is by being still. Achieving this state is the goal of spiritual practices.

Spiritual practices train you to be still, to be quiet inside, so that you can experience your true nature. Being still is not natural to human beings because you have an ego. To get out of the prison created by the ego, it is necessary to do what the ego has been steering you away from all your life: Be still.

Being still is about cultivating a quieter mind. Keeping the body still and slowing down the breath are part of most spiritual practices, because a relaxed body makes quieting the mind easier. Taking time to just sit and do nothing is central to experiencing inner stillness and sets the stage for the important practice of meditation.

There is nothing like the practice of meditation to quiet the mind. Although you will never completely quiet the mind as long as you are human, meditation gives you a fighting chance against the momentum and compelling nature of thought. A regular practice of meditation makes detaching from your thoughts easier, because meditation turns the volume down on your thoughts so that you can better attune to what is real and disregard what is false (thought).

Consciousness is always experiencing. Often it is lost in thought and the experience created by thought, like being lost in a movie in which you are the central character. Consciousness gets lost in the imaginary world of your mind. When consciousness is not lost in thought, it is attending to the sensory experience in the here and now and to more subtle input, such as intuitions or feelings of gratitude or peace. When you are not being run by the imaginary world of your mind, actions naturally flow in response to sensory and other more subtle input, much of which is overlooked when the focus is primarily on the egoic mind.

When you are attuned to the here and now, you might find yourself responding to an intuition, a creative idea, a loving feeling, an urge to act, or an inspiration. Responding to such things is intrinsically rewarding because they arise from a deep, true place within your being, one untainted by self-interest, fear, or a sense of lack.

Attuning to stillness leads to living life in a new, more fulfilling way, to action that is not centered around *me, my life,* and *my needs,* but action that naturally flows from the joy of just being. You experience yourself as a flow of being rather than someone who is this or that or who needs this or that or who wants this or that. You just are, and who knows what you will do next and where that will lead? And you do not need to know.

This is a frightening prospect to the ego. The ego does not want a life like that! Maybe this is how you feel as well. Words cannot adequately describe what the life of a butterfly is like. But if you were to experience it, you would know the rightness of living in such a way and you would not return to being a caterpillar.

The proof of the goodness and rightness of this direction—away from a life determined by the egoic mind and toward one governed by stillness, or joy—is that people do not return to the old way of the caterpillar once they know freedom and joy, if they can help it. Freedom may be scary to the ego, but it is inarguably preferable. Moreover, it is your destiny.

To become still is a matter of learning to listen to something other than your thoughts. To listen means to be receptive to. You listen to life, to what is here and now. Cultivating stillness is a matter of being receptive to what is real and true here and now. What is being experienced now? Without placing any evaluations or judgments on it, you simply experience what is arising in the here and now, drink it in or let it pass through, as it may. Noticing what is, touching it gently with your awareness, without clinging or pushing it away, is the way of stillness. This is also a description of meditation.

To be still is to just be. Be and experience what is here right now. You *are* the experience of right now. This experience might include thoughts and feelings, but when you are grounded in stillness, your experience of life is not overshadowed by the imaginary world of the mind. Thoughts and feelings are noticed, appreciated for what they are, embraced, blessed, and kissed good-bye. Everything passes in its own time. When you are still, you let everything come and everything go in its own time. You just *be* and let it all be as it is.

THE NINTH TEACHING

Let Everything Be

Everything is the way it is, and everything is in constant change. Nothing stays the same. This is the truth. This is the reality. It is a reality that the ego is not comfortable with, because the ego cannot control the natural flow of life, as the ego would like. The ego is determined to have its way with life, but sheer will is not enough. Life will move as it will. People have some influence on this movement; they are a factor in the flow. But they do not determine the flow, which is already established to some extent by a grand design.

Many have likened life to a river, and this is a good metaphor. The river is more powerful and enduring than anything or anyone on the river. It has a force of its own, independent of those traveling it, who cannot change the river's course but are obliged to follow it. Those on the river do have freedom to maneuver, however: They can paddle slowly or quickly or even try to buck the river. They can sing or they can cry. They can love or they can hate. What you choose to do while you are on the river affects the experience of being on the river, but not the river. So, too, with life: You have a choice about how you respond internally and externally to life, but you are not in control of what life brings, of how it shows up moment to moment.

Like life, the river is constantly moving and so is the scenery while traveling down the river. Every moment is a new moment, a new experience. The mind tries to hold on to some experiences, while it pushes others away, but that only affects how you experience the moment, not life itself.

Life continues to do what it does, just as the river does, whether you like it or not. So, the only thing you actually have control over is your attitude toward whatever is happening. Life is doing whatever it is doing, and you are either laughing or crying, accepting what is happening or hating it. Which will it be? What a different experience these two states are, and what a blessing that you have a choice! What if you didn't?

Often it does not feel like you have a choice to smile instead of cry, to accept instead of rail against. It seems this way because you have an ego that automatically resists rather than accepts. Of course, something else within you is always in acceptance. When you are able to align with that, you drop into the flow and you are happy: You merrily row your boat down the stream.

How can the key to happiness be this simple when being happy seems so difficult sometimes? The illusion spun by the mind is very powerful and convincing. You are often quite sure that it is impossible to be happy with the way things are, and you have lots of reasons for why this is so. But does your case against life change anything? Does being unhappy and resisting life change anything? Of course not.

Since you cannot control the way things are, the only solution—the *only* one—is to surrender to the way they are, which means giving up the struggle and complaints. Your attitude toward the way things are is the only thing you have control over. This is such an important lesson. When you master this lesson, you will be happy and at peace. What would happen if everyone were happy and at peace on this planet? It would be wonderful to find out, wouldn't it? Will you do your part?

And so, the ninth teaching is *let everything be.* If you let everything be, that does not mean that things will not change, which is the fear the ego has about moments it does not like. When the ego hears "Let everything be," it assumes this means "Don't try to change what you don't like." But that is not the meaning at all, because of course things will change and quite likely you are meant to be part of that process of change. Letting everything be does not mean letting everything stay the way it is, because nothing stays the same anyway.

Let everything be means let life do what it is already doing. It is too late to change that anyway. Letting everything be is the only response that makes sense, since you have no other choice, except in regard to your attitude. Letting everything be is the rational choice. To make the rational choice, however, you have to align with something other than the irrational ego. The rational part of yourself is your higher nature.

When your attitude is to let everything be, this acceptance allows you to relax and feel at peace with whatever is going on. What a relief it is to not have to fight with the way things are! How exhausting it is to feel angry, sad, or afraid. Acceptance keeps you in the flow instead of thrashing about and possibly drowning, which is how tempestuous emotions feel. Instead of being upset and overwhelmed, you relax and let everything be as it is. Life is much easier that way. Thrashing never helped anyway.

Acceptance is moving in the direction that life is going. If it goes left, you go left; if it goes right, you go right; if it stops, you stop. You take your cue from life, which is always showing you exactly what it wants. Does it want you to win? Then you win. Does it want you to fail? Then you fail. Whether you win or fail gracefully is the part that is up to you.

If you accept the direction in which life is moving, then you will surely act gracefully. Acceptance allows you to align with your true nature. From there, you respond to life with love, courage, patience, strength, and wisdom. If you are able to accept what life brings, you fall into a place of grace, where you experience the beneficence and bounty of life, and all you know is gratitude. Acceptance brings the rewards you long for, while non-acceptance, bucking the river, reaps only suffering. This is how life teaches and guides you. You learn to go in the direction that rewards you with joy, peace, and love.

These good feelings are proof that goodness underlies life, because when you align with acceptance, joy, peace, and love, you are rewarded. When you do not, you suffer. The barometer that indicates when you are aligned with the ego instead of your higher nature is suffering. It is a warning signal that tries to get your attention to tell you something. "What is my suffering trying to tell me now?" you might ask. "How am I saying no to life instead of yes?"

Every time you suffer, you are supposing something: "Things are supposed to be different. I am supposed to be different. She is supposed to be different. The past is supposed to be different. I am supposed to feel differently." All of these suppositions are false. You decided how things are supposed to be, you tried to make them that way, and when they turned out differently, you felt angry or sad. The truth is that everything is just as it is "supposed" to be. There is nothing ever wrong with life, only with your beliefs about it. What a miracle it is to discover this. What a relief! You can just relax and let life be as it is, let yourself be as you are, and let others be as they are. However life is showing up is how it is supposed to show up. To assume anything else is to suffer.

Your ego is accustomed to saying no to life. It was built to say no to life. To counteract this tendency, you can choose to say yes in the midst of your ego's resistance and rejection of life. You can notice the mind's complaints and then remind yourself that all is well and unfolding as it needs to. This is the truth.

When you counter a lie, such as "All is *not* well," with the truth, "All is well," you neutralize and diffuse the power of the lie. If you do this often enough, those lies will cease to arise in your mind. This is how the egoic mind is transformed. The lies are seen for what they are and the truth is declared instead. Choose to say yes in the midst of the ego's no, and that no will become a whisper and eventually disappear. Even if the ego's no does not disappear completely, it will be impotent and unable to affect your state of consciousness.

How do you say yes when something in you is screaming no? There is something within you that is already saying—and feeling—yes. Choosing to say yes in the midst of the ego's no will put you in contact with your true nature, which embraces life no matter what is happening. Although the ego's no can be overpowering at times, another, quieter voice is always saying yes.

Find that voice of acceptance. Look for it. Listen for it. And then give your attention to it, and it will become louder. If you give your attention to the no, then the no will continue to drown out the yes. You have to choose yes over no or you will not move beyond the ego's grasp. What chooses yes over no? That is your true nature. Empower it rather than the ego. Let the voice of love, peace, and wisdom prevail.

THE TENTH TEACHING

Let Love Be Your Guide

That love is the highest value is indisputable. Only someone who has been deprived of love might dispute this out of his or her woundedness; and yet, love is the only thing that can heal such woundedness. Love is that powerful and pervasive a force. It is, in fact, the only force in the universe. And that is very good news.

Words are inadequate to describe this force. If you call it love, it becomes limited to the realm of human emotions. But the emotion of love is a poor reflection of the force I am speaking about. This force as it moves through the human being gets corrupted by self-interest and greed. Love becomes something you have to get from someone else and something you never have enough of, like everything the ego seeks. This is not love but a lack of love masquerading as love. Neediness is a better word for it.

Neediness is the opposite of love, for true love results in a natural outpouring of love to others, not in desiring anything from them. You can pretend to love others in hopes of getting what you want and you can love them because they give you what you want or because you imagine that they will, but this is the ego's version of love, and it stems from need.

When you are connected to the force that governs the universe, you are naturally loving, and this is its own reward. You need nothing from anyone. Love is a state of completion, not need. It is a state of giving, not taking. From this sense of completion flows an adoration of and generosity toward all life. When you feel complete and at peace, you are full of love, gratitude, and joy. This state is what everyone longs for.

The ego does not know how to achieve this state. The things the ego does to try to attain this state only take one deeper into egoic consciousness, which is a state of lack and fear in which love cannot flow and peace does not exist. You can only achieve a state of peace and love by seeing that nothing is lacking within you, within others, or within life, that everything is already good and as it is meant to be. All is well and unfolding as it needs to, and love is what is behind this unfolding. Love is all that exists.

To the ego, this sounds flowery and untrue. That love is behind all of life and that life is good is difficult for human beings to comprehend. It is not how the mind sees things, and the mind is what tries to comprehend this. But the mind will never be able to understand the nature of life or the nature of love. The truth about life is so far beyond the mind that the mind is inadequate to the task. But that does not change the truth.

Despite the difficulty of the mind to know the truth, the truth is known to you in your heart of hearts. You know the love that is at your core, and often you obey and honor it. When you are aligned with it, you are happy and at peace; when you are not, you are not happy and at peace. You know this much: Love is what you want, not a love that needs but a love that forgets itself in the presence of the beloved, which is all of life.

This self-forgetfulness is love. What is the self that is forgotten? It is the false self. When you move beyond all ideas of yourself, all images, and the sense of yourself as someone who is this or that, you fall in love with life. And you discover that you *are* life. No longer does anything separate you from life. You lose your boundaries, as the *you* that you thought you were falls away, and all that remains is the spaciousness of your being.

The being that you are is the same being that everyone is. Beingness flows everywhere, without boundaries that distinguish you from everyone else. Your being and everyone else's being are the same, merged into one! What a surprise, when previously you felt such a distinct sense of self. When this sense of self dissolves, you are left with your true nature, which is deeply in love with life and sees itself in all life. The joy you feel in this dissolving is the joy you have been looking for, but it was not to be found in riches, popularity, or acclaim. Your very being is the source of the exquisite joy you have been searching for.

How do you arrive at this place of exquisite joy? *Let love be your guide.* This is the tenth teaching. For as long as the ego has been your guide, it has taken you away from love. It is time to recognize this now and shift your allegiance. Once you realize the falseness of the guide you have been following and that there is another, truer guide, you can be on your way Home.

If you have a false guide, then no matter where it takes you, even if some of those places are pleasant, you will not arrive at your intended destination. No matter how convincing that guide is, it still cannot take you there. That is the human condition: The guide is very convincing but also false. It does not know the way, although it acts like it knows and other people are following it. But that does not change a thing—it does not know the way.

When you are trying to get somewhere and you do not succeed, that is painful. But once you know you are on the right path and that you *will* get there, you find the strength to overcome any challenges along the way. You feel strong, supported, uplifted, and confident in your steps. Being aligned with your true nature feels good and right, and that is enough.

On the other hand, following a false guide is like being stuck in brambles. The path hurts, and it is difficult to summon the courage and strength to continue. When you are not aligned with your true nature, nothing ever feels like enough. You are never satisfied and you can never rest. But that is as it is meant to be. You are not meant to find the wrong path rewarding.

Let love be your guide means align with the divine force of love within you and let it move you in your life. When you were aligned with the false guide, it moved you by scaring you and telling you that you needed something else to be happy. It used a stick and a carrot to move you. With love as your guide, you act because it is intrinsically joyful to act. Acting, when that action is aligned with being, is its own reward.

Let love be your guide also means let love be your master, let it guide your actions and speech. Be the servant of love. Do your actions and speech come from love? If not, do not engage in them. Do your actions and speech lead to greater love between you and others? If not, do not engage in them. Will you be a force for love on this planet? One individual acting as a force for love can counteract hundreds, even thousands, acting otherwise. You are powerful.

What you do matters. How you act and what you say matters. Be the loving force you can be. This is my final teaching.

THE TEN TEACHINGS

THE FIRST TEACHING
Open and Receive

You only need to see that love and guidance are already present in every moment for this to be your experience and your reality. If you find this love and guidance difficult to perceive, then merely express your openness and willingness to perceiving and receiving it. Also be willing to see yourself as the divine being that you truly are—and you will be! That is the promise. You can be what you truly are when you open to that possibility and are willing to know yourself as that.

THE SECOND TEACHING
Acknowledge the Hand of Grace

To connect with your Source and the goodness and love at your core, it is necessary to notice and acknowledge that the Divine is immanent and operative in your life and in every life. You are deeply loved and guided in every moment by that which created you and lives in you and through you. If you do not see the truth of this, you will accept your mind's conclusions about life. These conclusions will not serve you.

THE THIRD TEACHING
Declare Your Deepest Desire

You and the spiritual forces that support your evolution will jointly bring peace and love into your life when you declare that you want these things more than anything else. Feel the depth and power of this desire and let it fuel your will to give peace and love your attention.

THE FOURTH TEACHING
Accept Life as It Is

It is impossible to love or feel at peace unless you accept life as it is. Non-acceptance closes the heart, which is the doorway to love and peace. There is no other way but acceptance to open that door. When you accept, peace comes and love can flow once again. Listening to the mind ensures that the heart will stay closed. If you take the mind's perspective as yours, then you will be at odds with life.

THE FIFTH TEACHING
Realize That Your Thoughts
and Feelings Are Not Yours

The human condition is a state of suffering for the simple reason that people do not naturally question their thoughts and feelings. They assume that their thoughts are valid, and they assume that their thoughts are *their* thoughts. These are mistaken assumptions, which lead to so much pain. These assumptions are at the root of human suffering. What if your thoughts and feelings were not yours?

THE SIXTH TEACHING
Be with What Is Real

Once you learn to disengage from your thoughts and feelings, all that is left is to be with what is real. This is the basis for a new life as a butterfly, a newly awakened human being. Once the false and unreal, or illusory, is disregarded, all that is left is what is real. What *is* real? Look around. What is it you can see and touch and feel and smell and taste? That is real. Without your senses, there is no world to experience, although consciousness still exists. So, consciousness is also real. These things: sensory experience and consciousness make up the world of the butterfly.

THE SEVENTH TEACHING
Follow Your Joy

Your place in the grand design is revealed by joy. Joy is the guiding force in butterfly consciousness. You are meant to be a butterfly, and joy is how you become one. Find the joy within you—that *is* you! Then go where that joy wants to go, do what that joy wants to do, and say what that joy wants to say. Being a butterfly is as simple as that. The mind wants to complicate this with "what ifs," but there is never a good reason to not follow your joy.

THE EIGHTH TEACHING
Be Still

To get out of the prison created by the ego, it is necessary to do what the ego has been steering you away from all your life: Be still. In between each and every thought is a space, and that is where freedom lies. In this space, it is possible—indeed, probable—that you will experience who you really are. Without taking time to be still, who you really are will be merely an intellectual understanding, not a living realization, and you will not know your joy.

THE NINTH TEACHING
Let Everything Be

Letting everything be does not mean letting everything stay the way it is, because nothing stays the same anyway. Let everything be means let life do what it is already doing. It is too late to change that anyway. Letting everything be is the only response that makes sense, since you have no other choice, except in regard to your attitude. You have a choice about how you will respond internally and externally to life, but you are not in control of what life brings, of how it shows up moment to moment.

THE TENTH TEACHING
Let Love Be Your Guide

Let love be your guide means align with the divine force of love within you and let it move you in your life. Let love be your guide also means let love be your master, let it guide your actions and speech. Be the servant of love. Do your actions and speech come from love? If not, do not engage in them. Do your actions and speech lead to greater love between you and others? If not, do not engage in them. How you act and what you say matters. Be the loving force you can be.

About the Author

Gina Lake is a nondual spiritual teacher and the author of over twenty books about awakening to one's true nature. She is also a gifted intuitive and channel with a master's degree in Counseling Psychology and over twenty-five years' experience supporting people in their spiritual growth. In 2012, Mother Mary and Jesus began dictating books through her. These teachings are based on universal truth, not on any religion. Her website offers information about her books and online courses, a free ebook, and audio and video recordings:

www.RadicalHappiness.com

Awakening Now Online Course

This course was created for your awakening. The methods presented are powerful companions on the path to enlightenment and true happiness. In this 100-day inner workout, you'll immerse yourself in materials, practices, guided meditations, and inquiries that will transform your consciousness. And in video webinars, you'll receive transmissions of Christ Consciousness. These transmissions are a direct current of love and healing that will help you break through to a new level of being. By the end of 100 days, you will have developed new habits and ways of being that will result in being more richly alive and present and greater joy and equanimity.

www.RadicalHappiness.com/courses

More Books by Gina Lake

Available in paperback, ebook, and audiobook formats.

From Stress to Stillness: Tools for Inner Peace. Most stress is created by how we think about things. *From Stress to Stillness* will help you to examine what you are thinking and change your relationship to your thoughts so that they no longer result in stress. Drawing from the wisdom traditions, psychology, New Thought, and the author's own experience as a spiritual teacher and counselor, *From Stress to Stillness* offers many practices and suggestions that will lead to greater peace and equanimity, even in a busy and stress-filled world.

Radical Happiness: A Guide to Awakening provides the keys to experiencing the happiness that is ever-present and not dependent on circumstances. This happiness doesn't come from getting what you want, but from wanting what is here now. It comes from realizing that who you think you are is not who you really are. This is a radical perspective! *Radical Happiness* describes the nature of the egoic state of consciousness and how it interferes with happiness, what awakening and enlightenment are, and how to live in the world after awakening.

Embracing the Now: Finding Peace and Happiness in What Is. The Now—this moment—is the true source of happiness and peace and the key to living a fulfilled and meaningful life. *Embracing the Now* is a collection of essays that can serve as daily reminders of the deepest truths. Full of clear insight and wisdom, *Embracing the Now* explains how the mind keeps us from being in the moment, how to move into the Now and stay there, and what living from the Now is like. It also explains how to overcome stumbling blocks to being in the Now, such as fears, doubts, misunderstandings, judgments, distrust of life, desires, and other conditioned ideas that are behind human suffering.

All Grace: New Teachings from Jesus on the Truth About Life. Grace is the mysterious and unseen movement of God upon creation, which is motivated by love and indistinct from love. *All Grace* was given to Gina Lake by Jesus and represents his wisdom and understanding of life. It is about the magnificent and incomprehensible force behind life, which created life, sustains it, and operates within it as you and me and all of creation. *All Grace* is full of profound and life-changing truth.

In the World but Not of It: New Teachings from Jesus on Embodying the Divine: From the Introduction, by Jesus: "What I have come to teach now is that you can embody love, as I did. You can become Christ within this human life and learn to embody all that is good within you. I came to show you the beauty of your own soul and what is possible as a human. I came to show you that it is possible to be both human and divine, to be love incarnate. You are equally both. You walk with one foot in the world of form and another in the Formless. This mysterious duality within your being is what this book is about." This book is another in a series of books dictated to Gina Lake by Jesus.

Choosing Love: Moving from Ego to Essence in Relationships. Having a truly meaningful relationship requires choosing love over your conditioning, that is, your ideas, fantasies, desires, images, and beliefs. *Choosing Love* describes how to move beyond conditioning, judgment, anger, romantic illusions, and differences to the experience of love and Oneness with another. It explains how to drop into the core of your Being, where Oneness and love exist, and be with others from there.

What Jesus Wants You to Know Today: About Himself, Christianity, God, the World, and Being Human: Jesus exists and has always existed to serve humanity, and one way he is doing this today is through this channel, Gina Lake, and others. In *What Jesus Wants You to Know Today,* Jesus answers many questions about his life and teachings and shares his perspective on the world. He brings his message of love, once again, to the world and corrects the record by detailing the ways that Christianity has distorted his teachings. He wants you to know that you, too, have the potential to be a Christ, to be enlightened as he was, and he explains how this is possible.

The Jesus Trilogy. In this trilogy by Jesus, are three jewels, each shining in its own way and illuminating the same truth: You are not only human but divine, and you are meant to flourish and love one another. In words that are for today, Jesus speaks intimately and directly to the reader of the secrets to peace, love, and happiness. He explains the deepest of all mysteries: who you are and how you can live as he taught long ago. The three books in *The Jesus Trilogy* were dictated to Gina Lake by Jesus and include *Choice and Will, Love and Surrender,* and *Beliefs, Emotions,* and *the Creation of Reality.*

A Heroic Life: New Teachings from Jesus on the Human Journey. The hero's journey—this human life— is a search for the greatest treasure of all: the gifts of your true nature. These gifts are your birthright, but they have been hidden from you, kept from you by the dragon: the ego. These gifts are the wisdom, love, peace, courage, strength, and joy that reside at your core. *A Heroic Life* shows you how to overcome the ego's false beliefs and face the ego's fears. It provides you with both a perspective and a map to help you successfully and happily navigate life's challenges and live heroically. This book is another in a series of books dictated to Gina Lake by Jesus.

Living in the Now: How to Live as the Spiritual Being That You Are. The 99 essays in *Living in the Now* will help you realize your true nature and live as that. They answer many questions raised by the spiritual search and offer wisdom on subjects such as fear, anger, happiness, aging, boredom, desire, patience, faith, forgiveness, acceptance, love, commitment, hope, purpose, meaning, meditation, being present, emotions, trusting life, trusting your Heart, and many other deep subjects. These essays will help you become more conscious, present, happy, loving, grateful, at peace, and fulfilled. Each essay stands on its own and can be used for daily contemplation.

Return to Essence: How to Be in the Flow and Fulfill Your Life's Purpose describes how to get into the flow and stay there and how to live life from there. Being in the flow and not being in the flow are two very different states. One is dominated by the ego-driven mind, which is the cause of suffering, while the other is the domain of Essence, the Divine within each of us. You are meant to live in the flow. The flow is the experience of Essence—your true self—as it lives life through you and fulfills its purpose for this life.

For more info, please visit the "Books" page at

www.RadicalHappiness.com